The Footie Coloring Book

This book is dedicated to all Footie/Footy/Rugby/Soccer/Football lovers.

Disclaimer: All characters, companies, events, places mentioned in the book are purely fictitious, any similarity with a person or company or

event or place is purely coincidental.

Introduction

Football and Rugby are loved by billions of people. There was a need for a football/footy/rugby/soccer coloring book. This book hopes to fill the big void created by lack of any coloring book in this space. It will reduce your stress and tension when your team ends up losing a game or two.

Please gift "The Footie Coloring Book" to your friends who are still following other games like cricket, etc. Make coloring great again by coloring all images in this book.

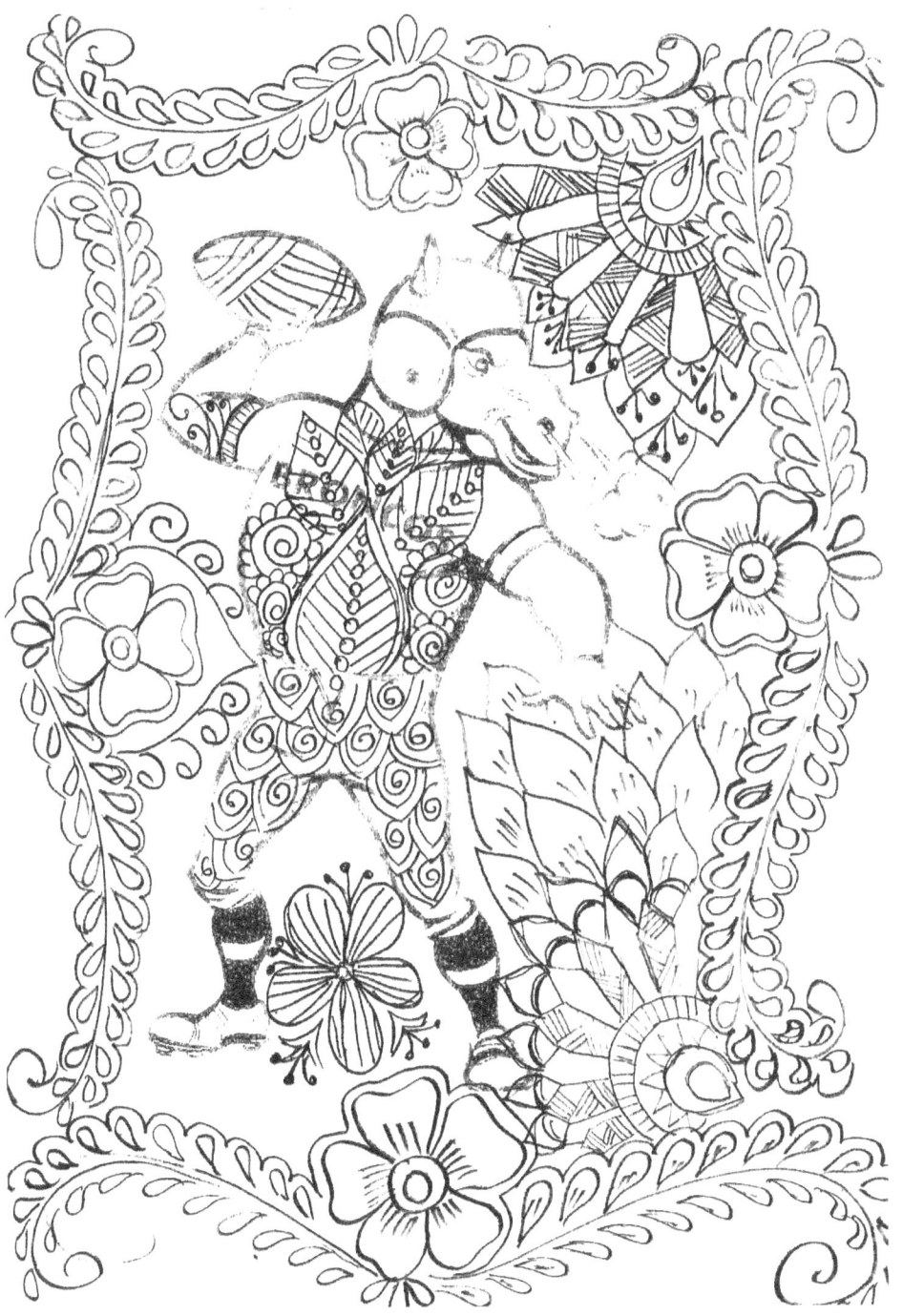

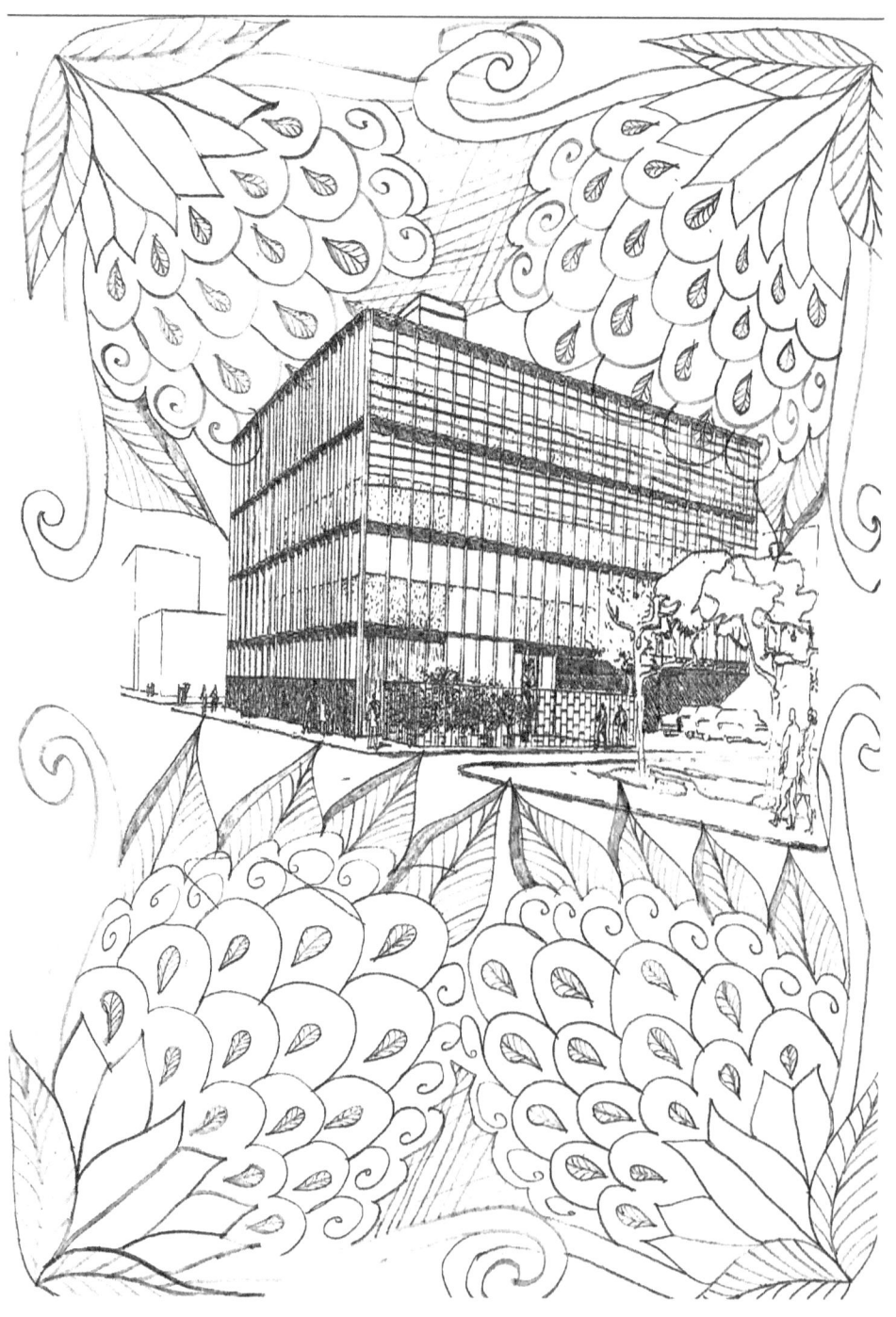

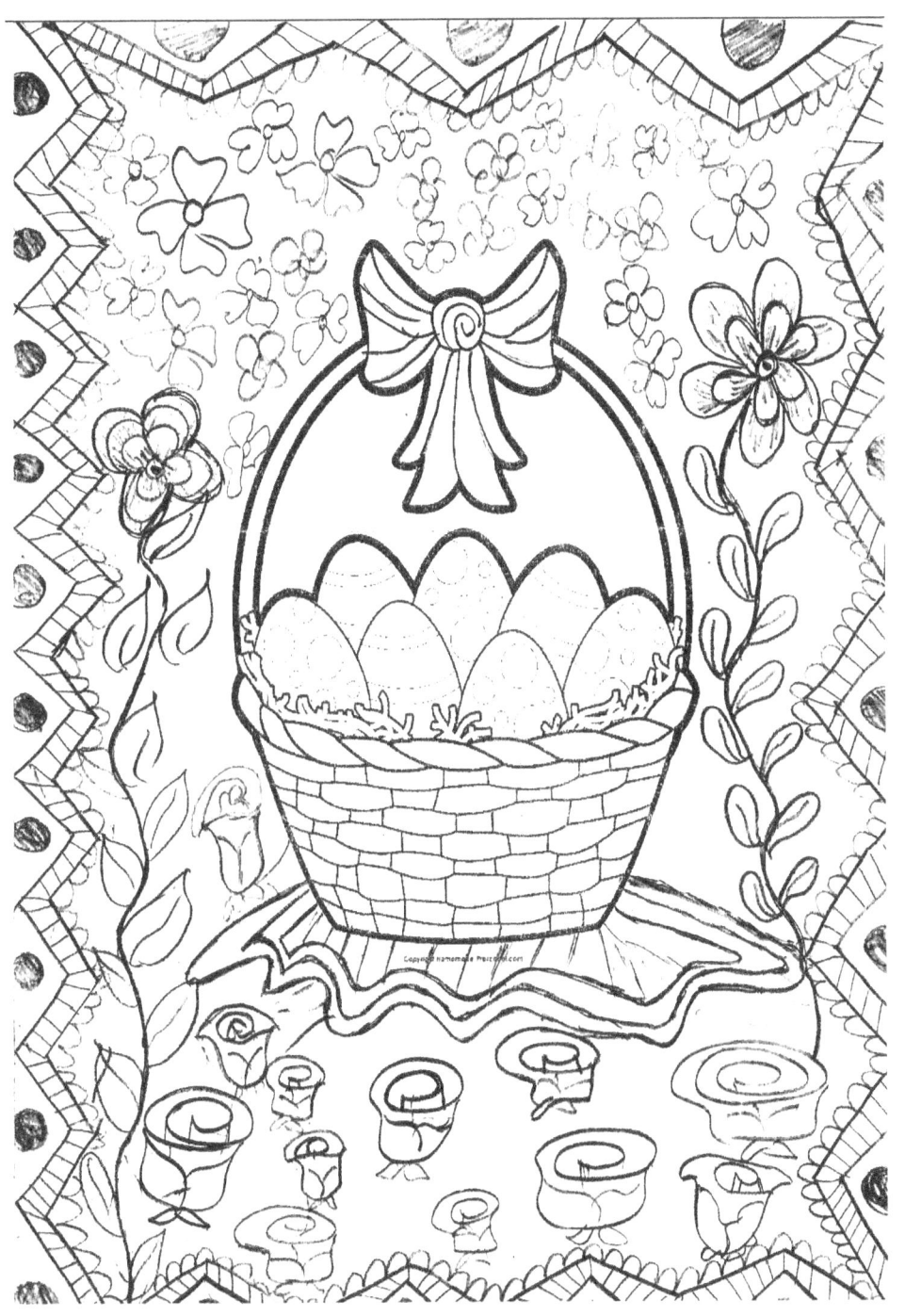

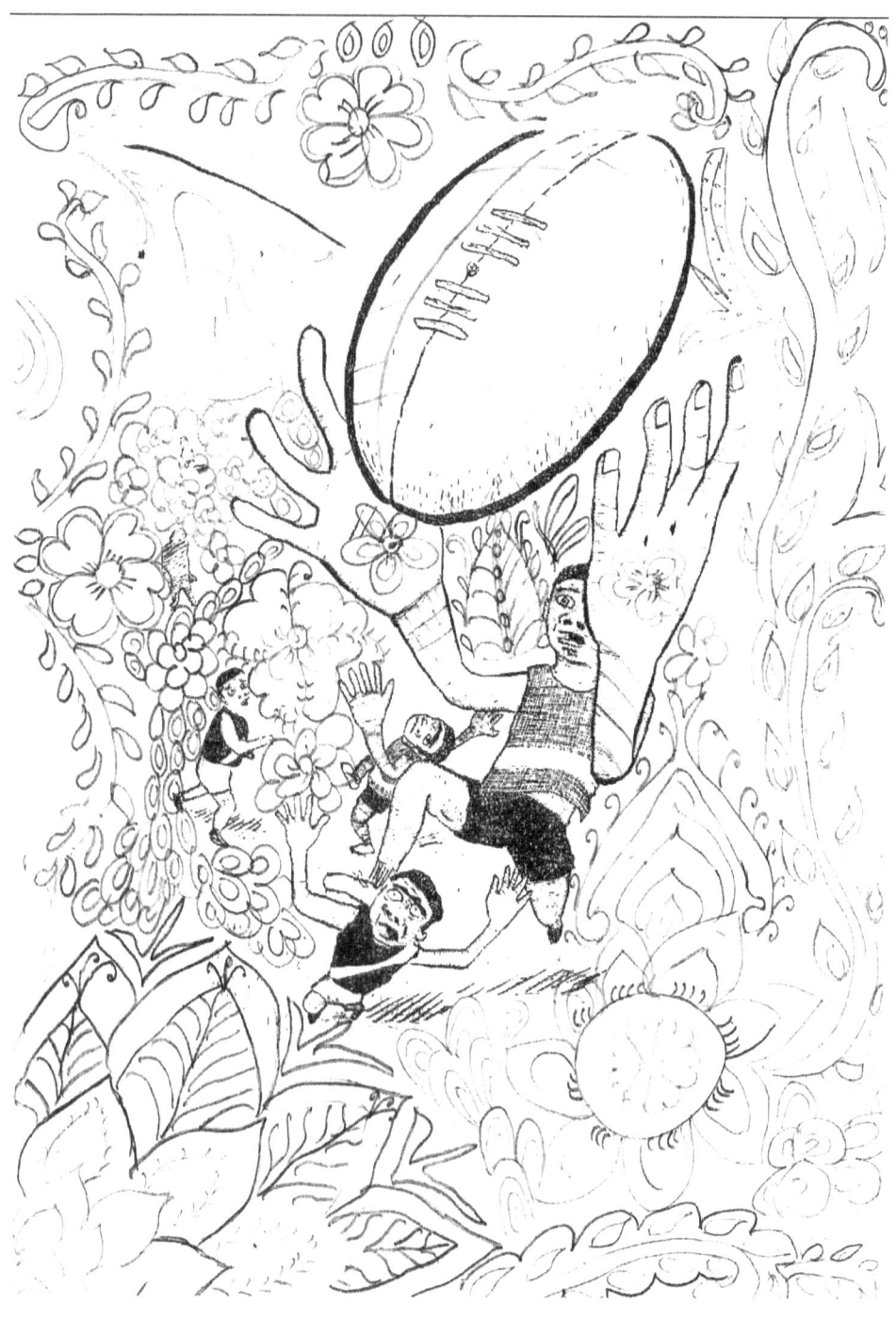

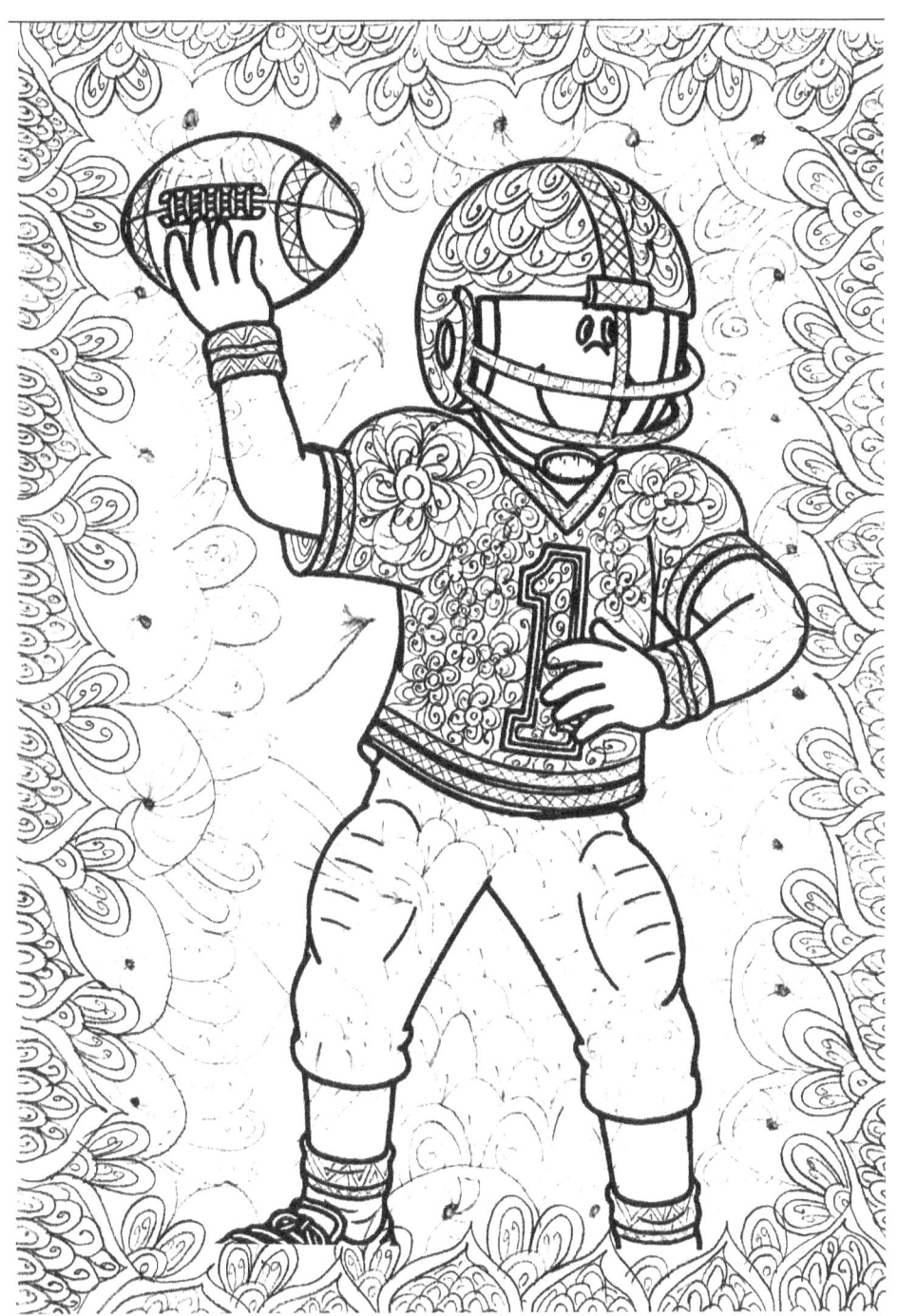

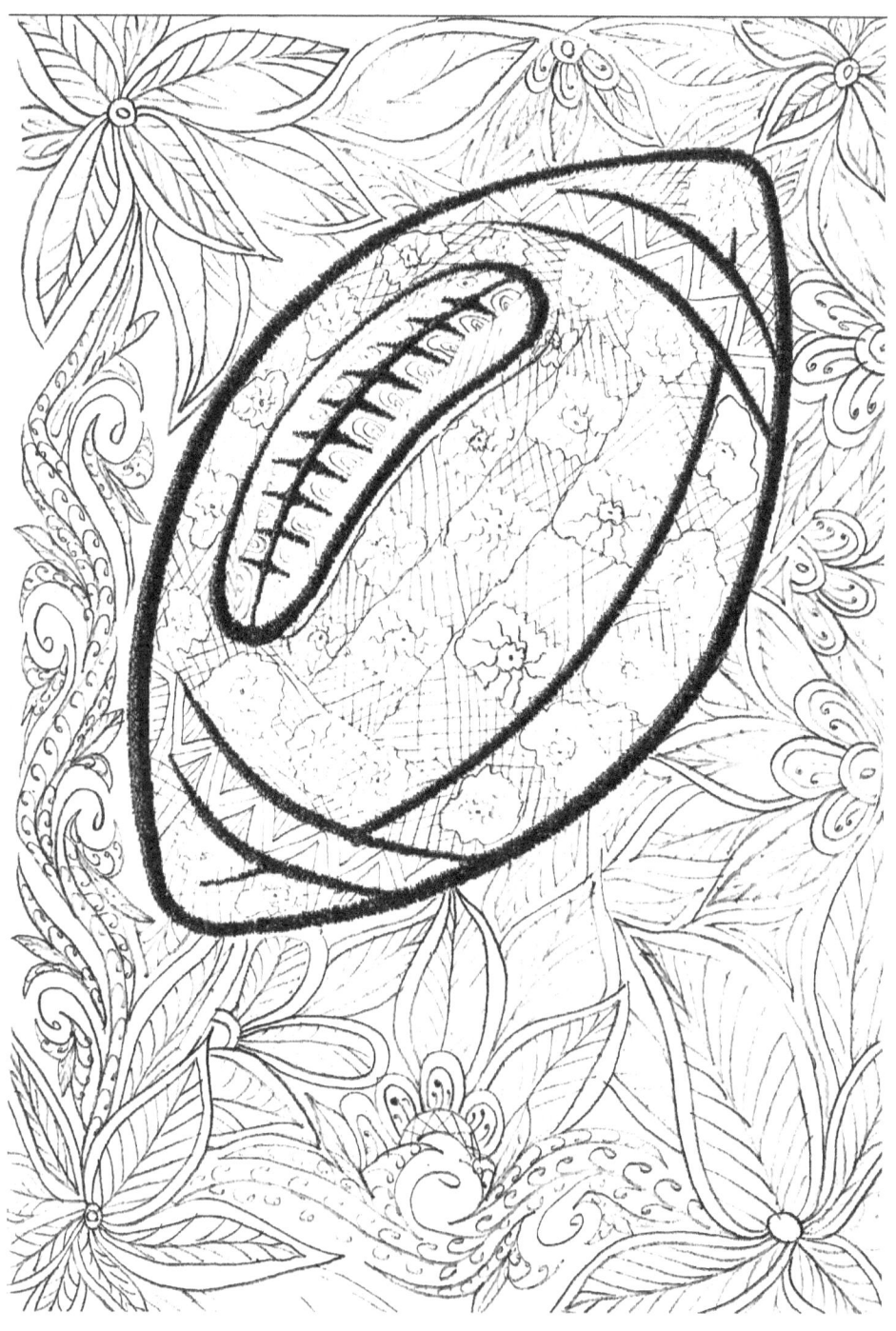

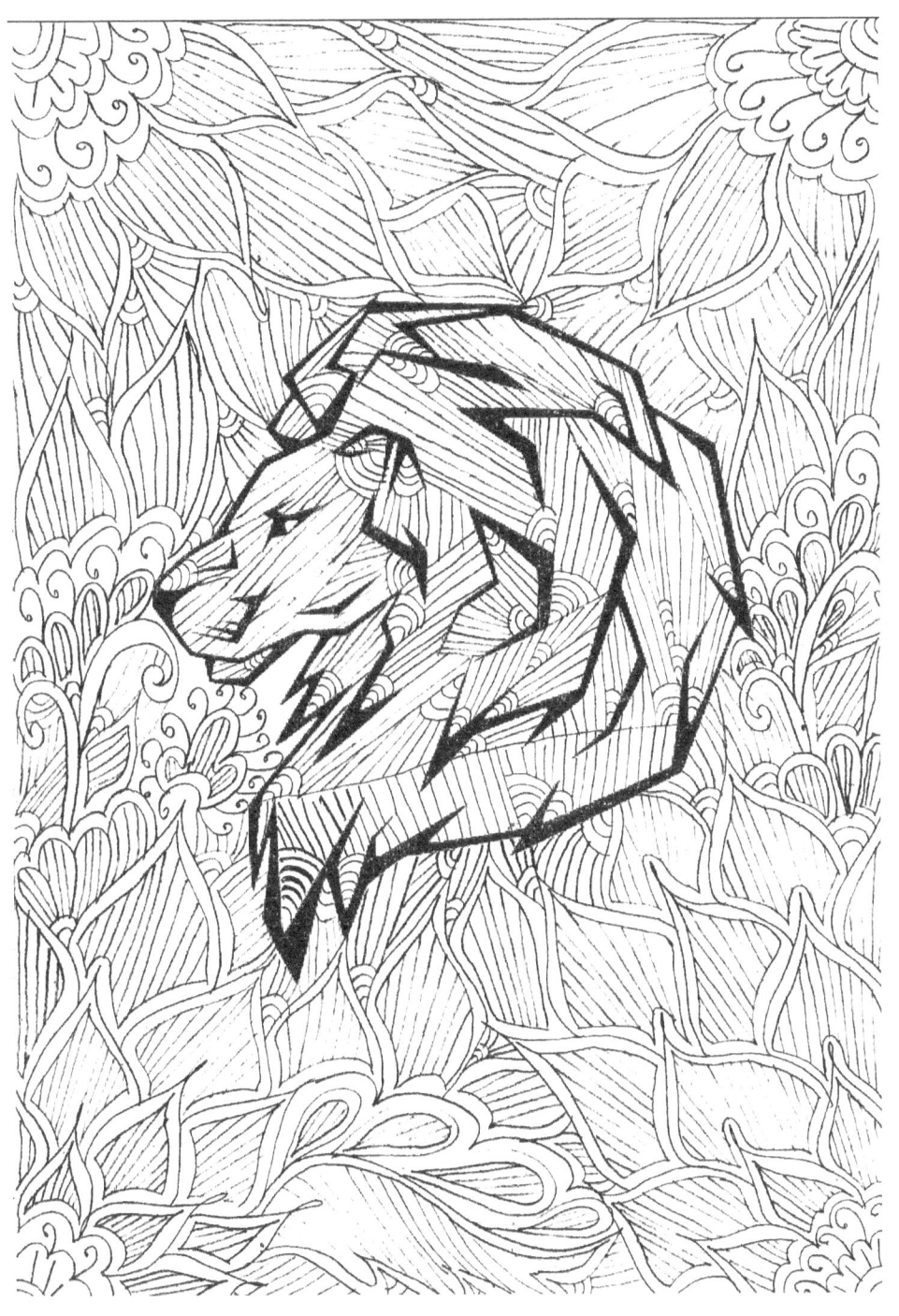

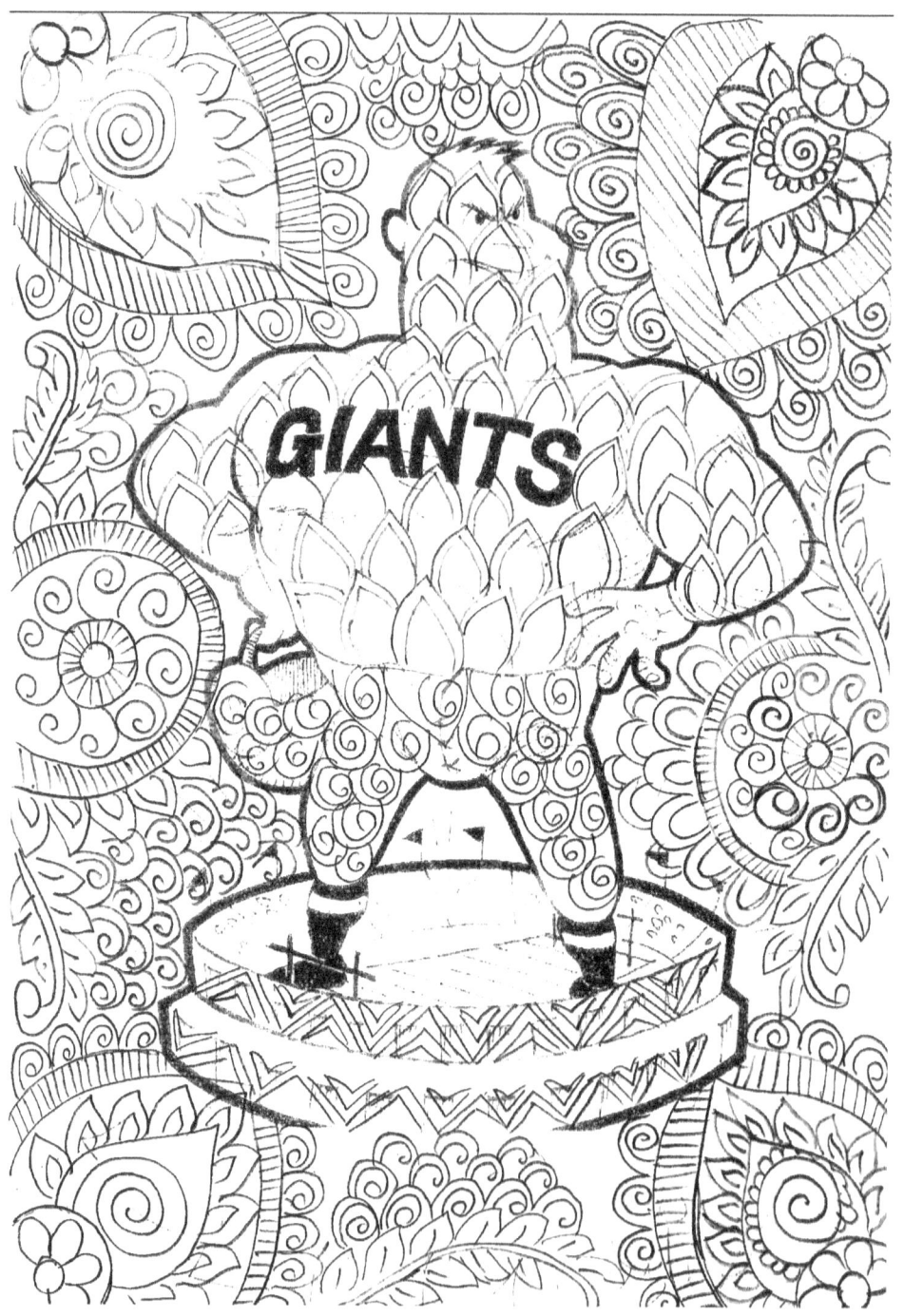

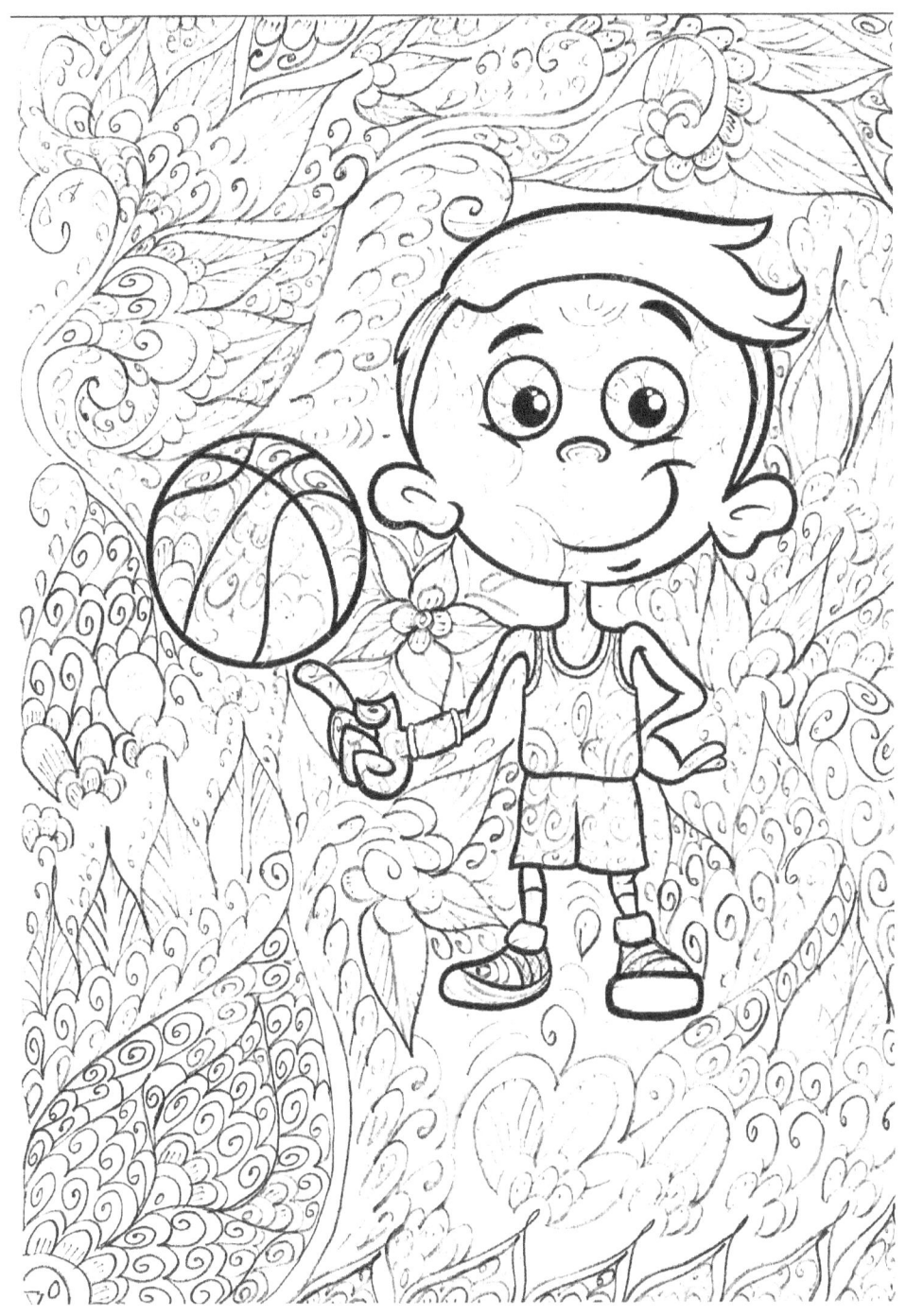

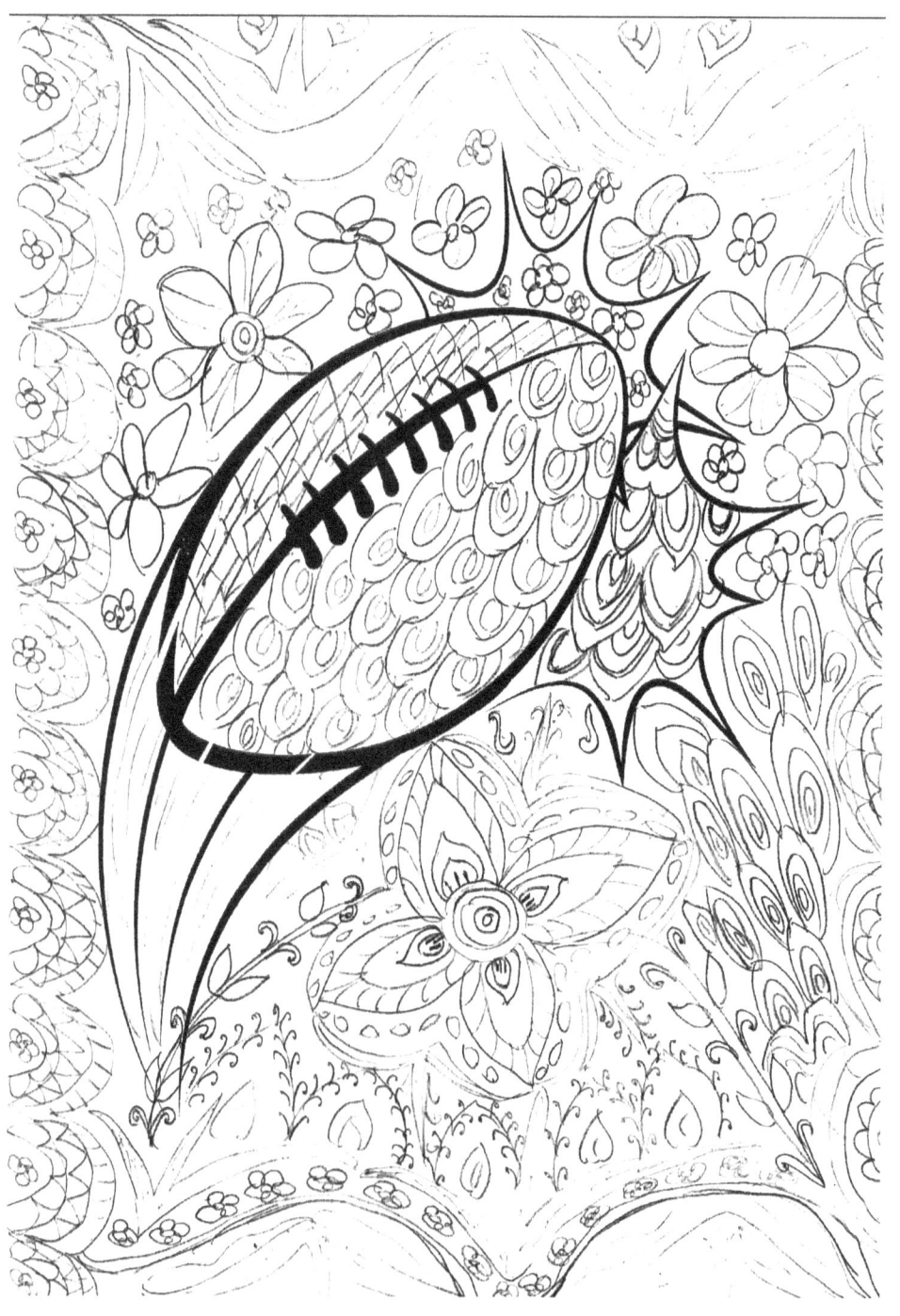

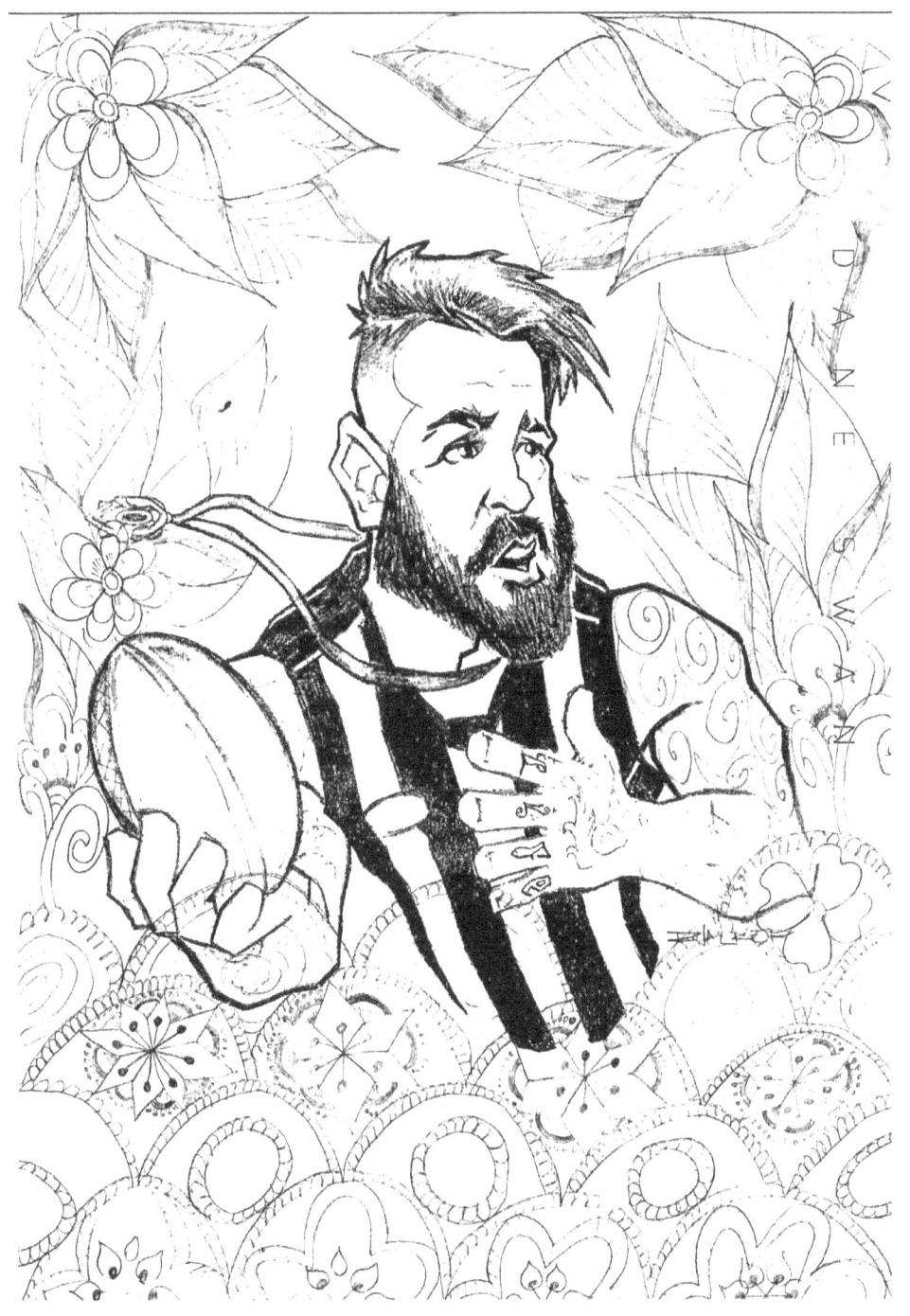

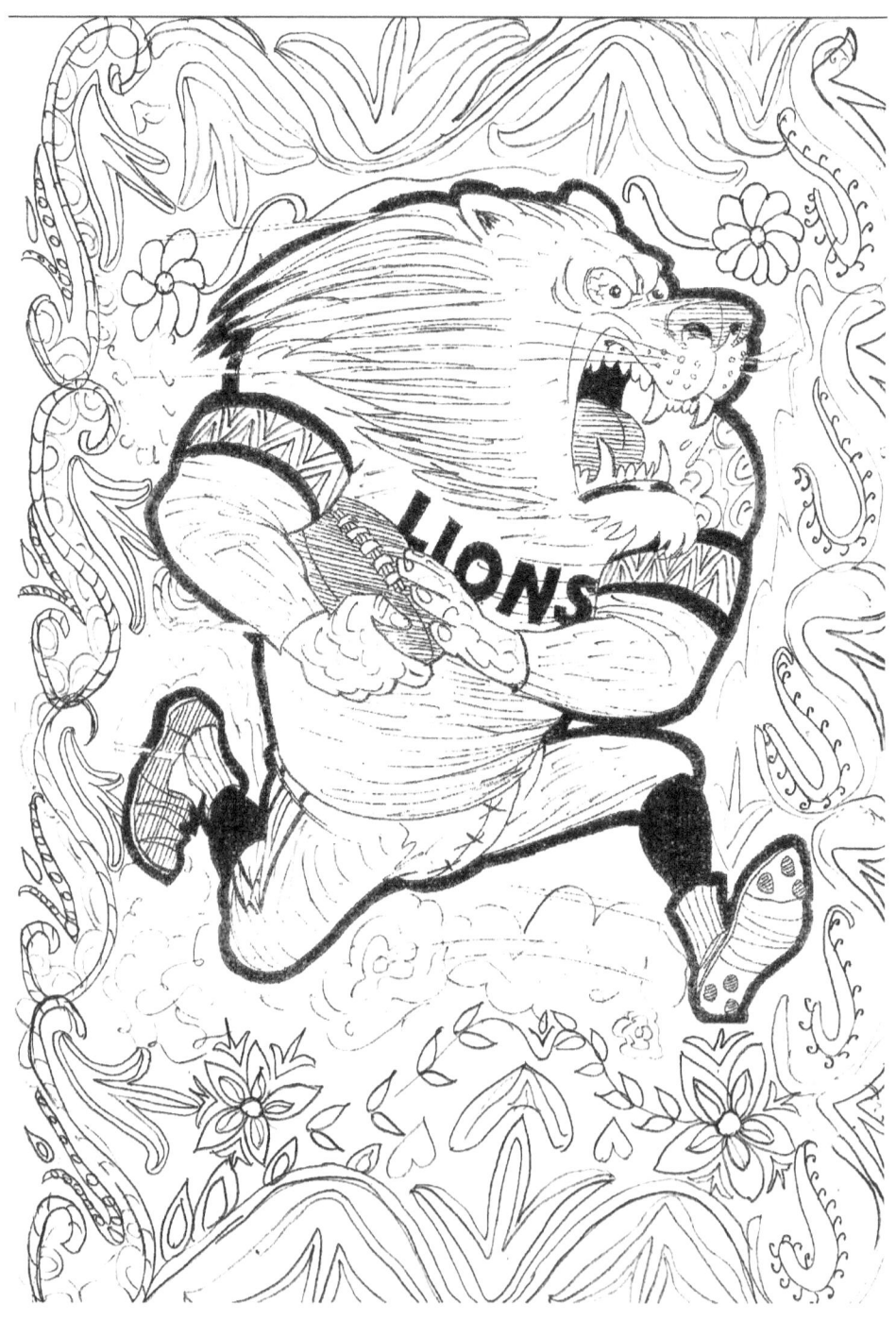

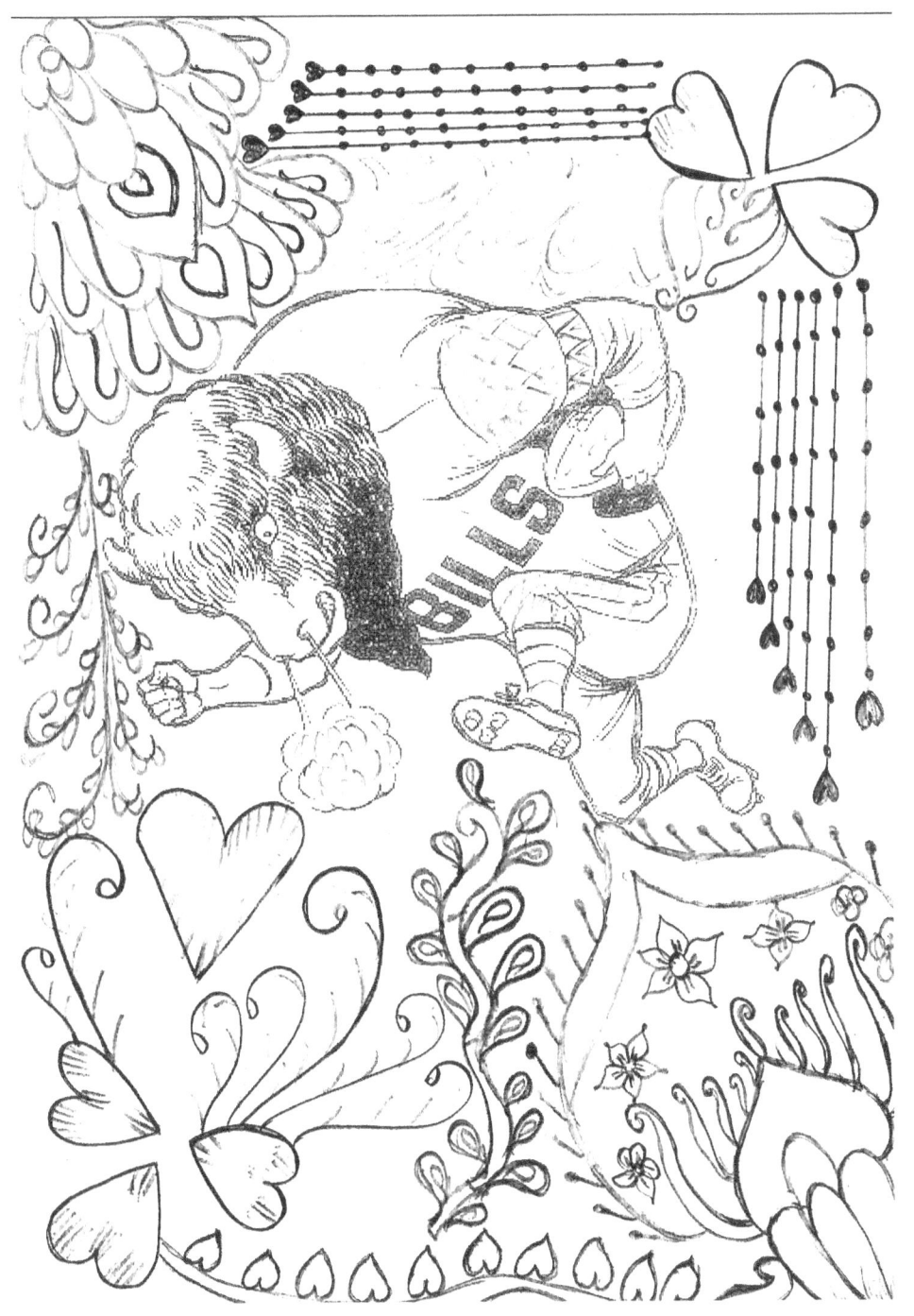

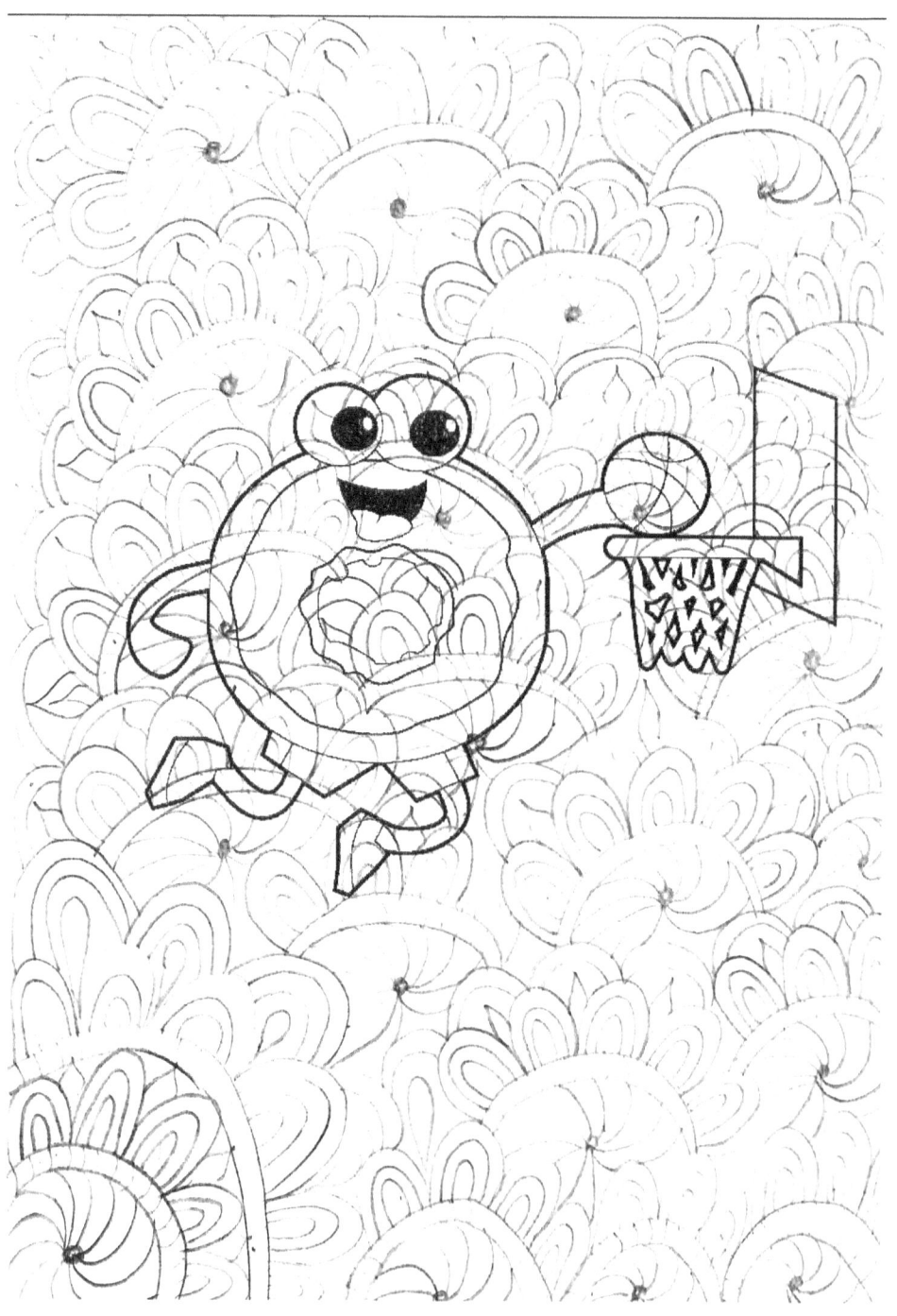

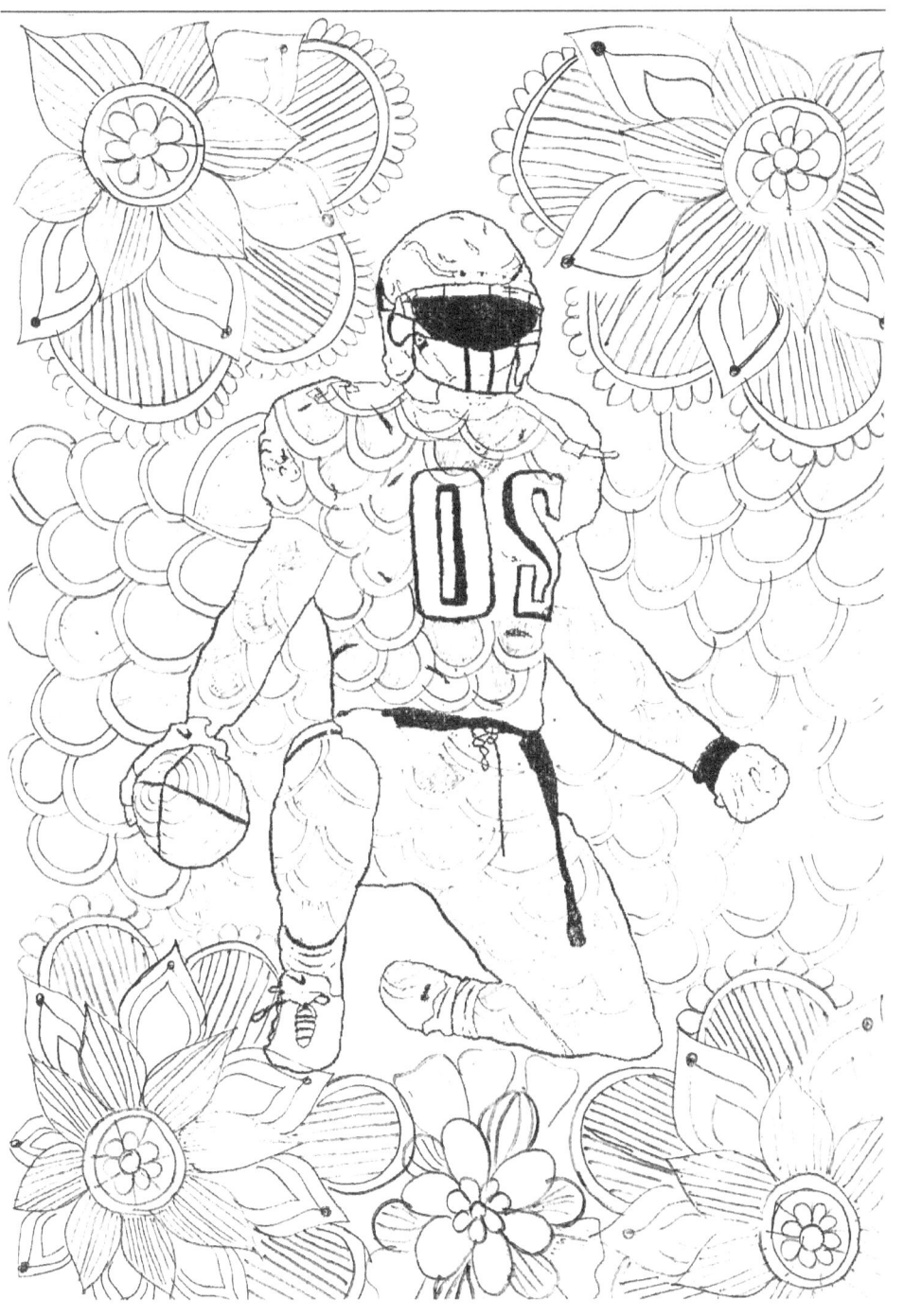

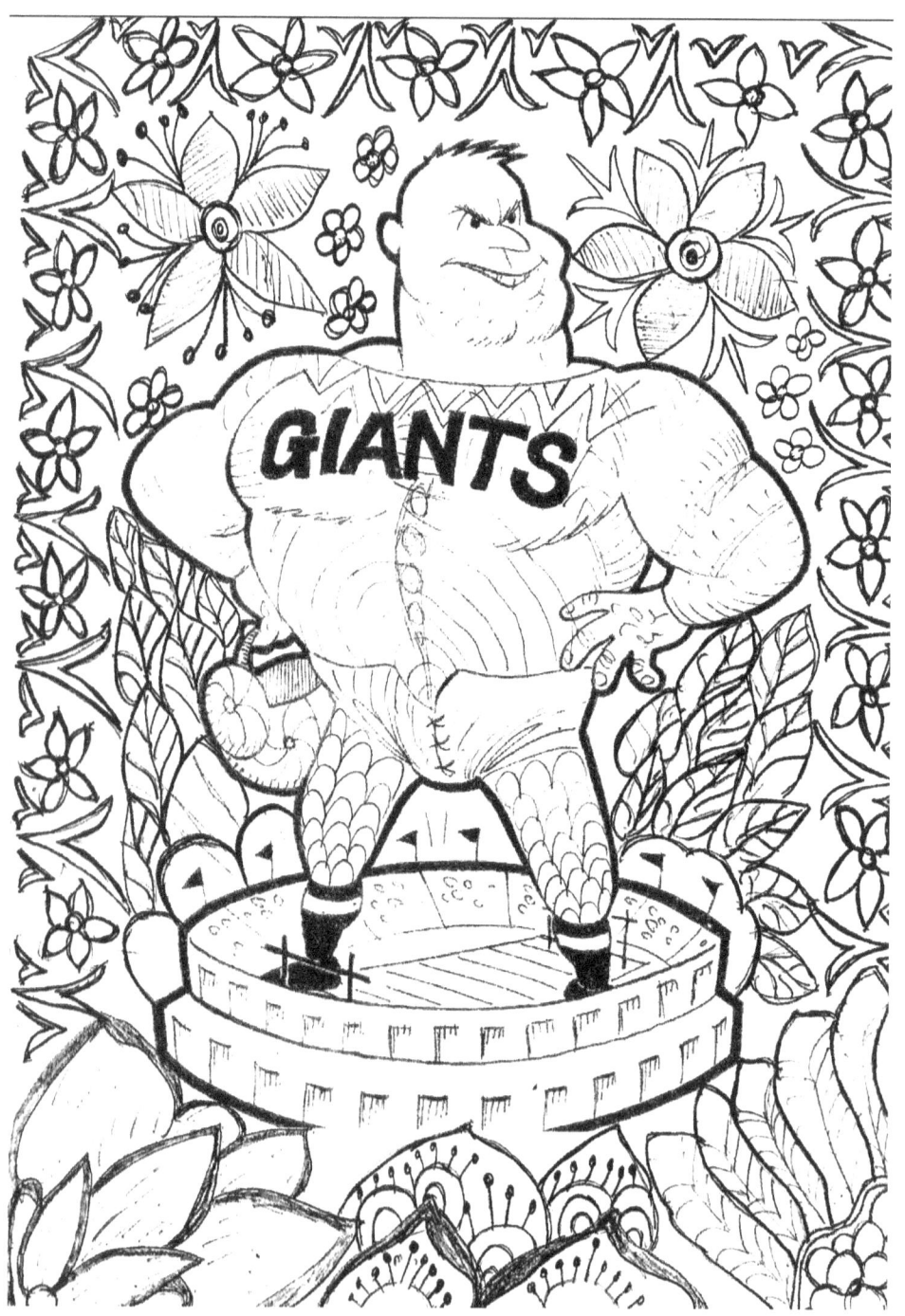

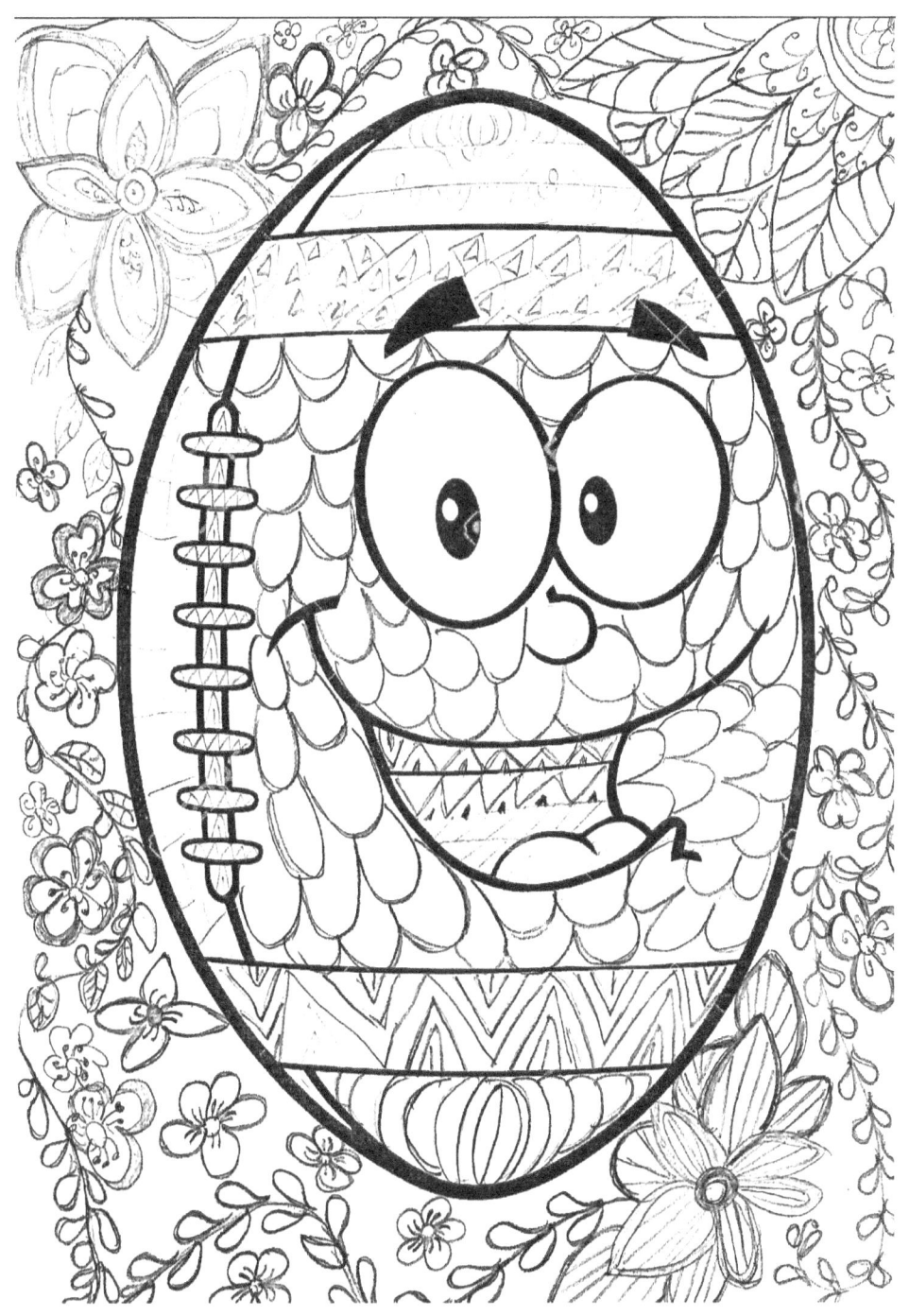

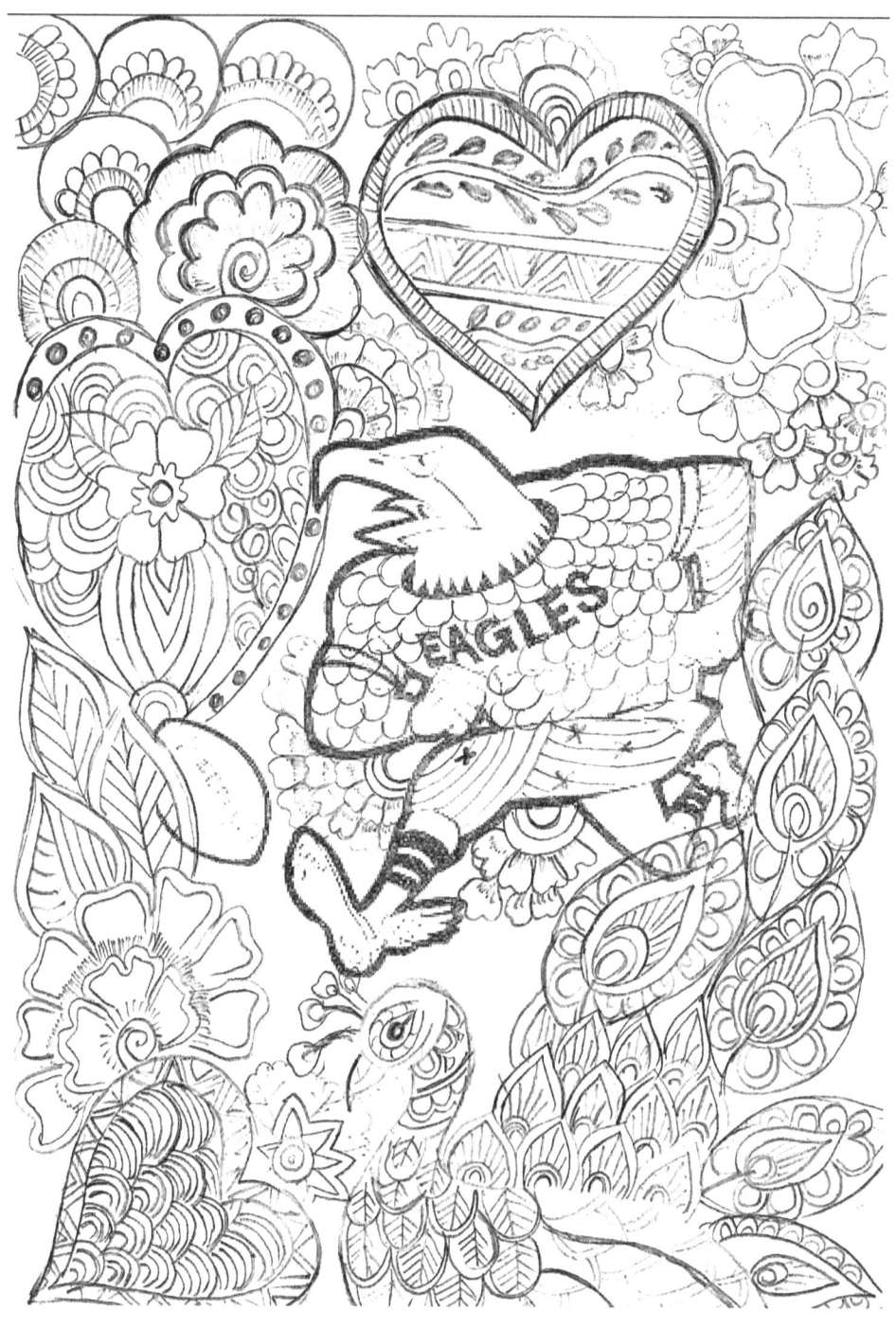

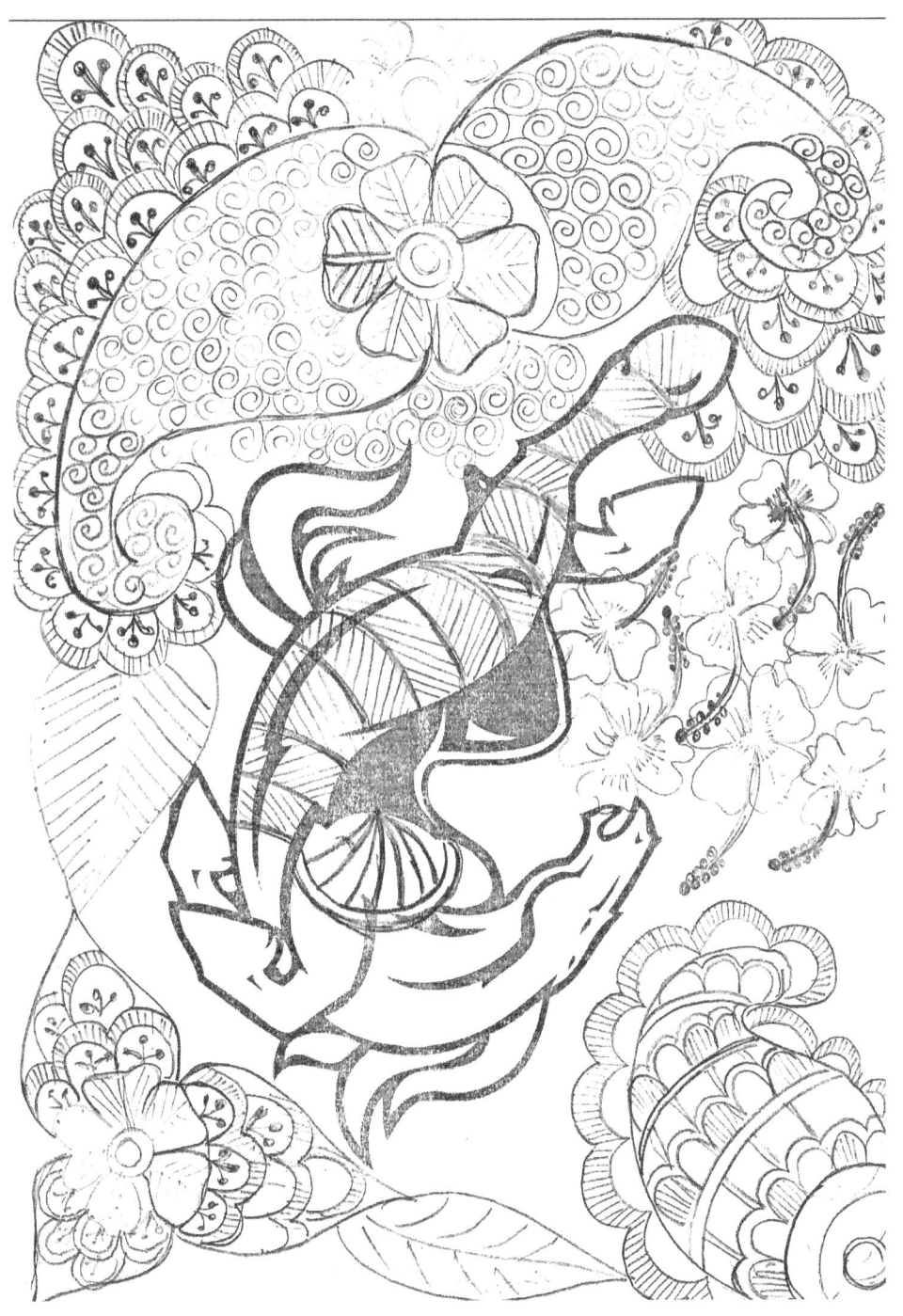

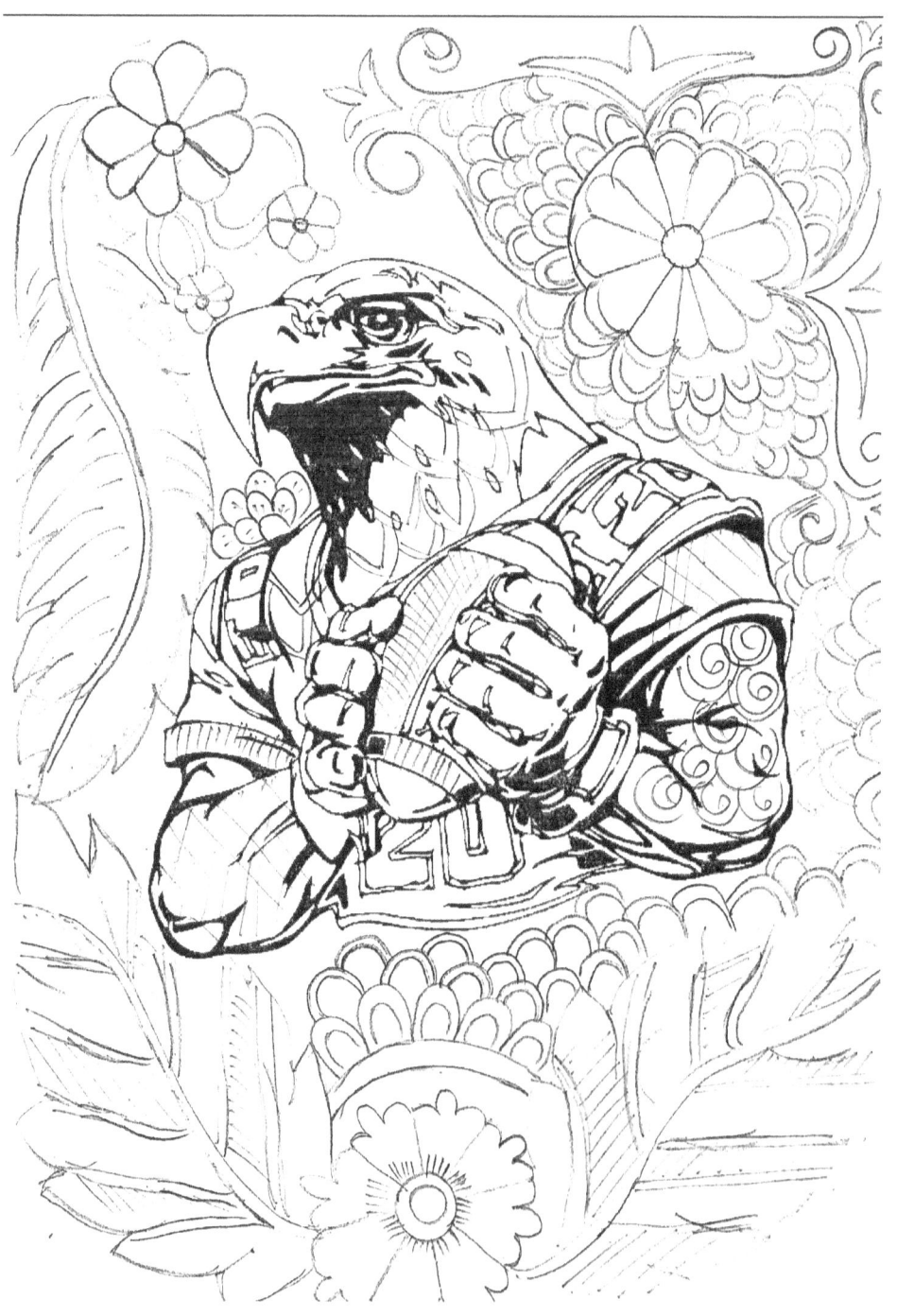

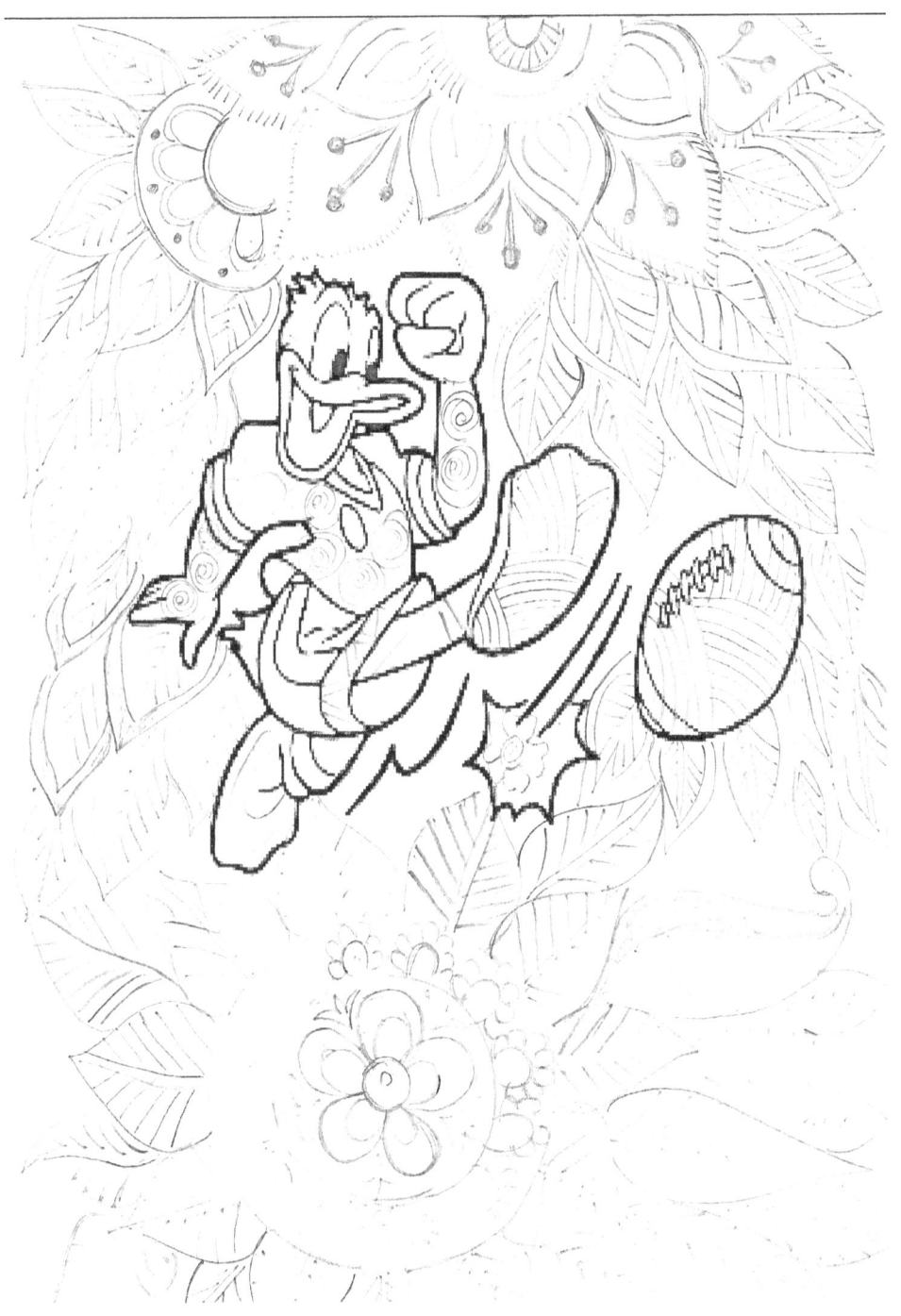

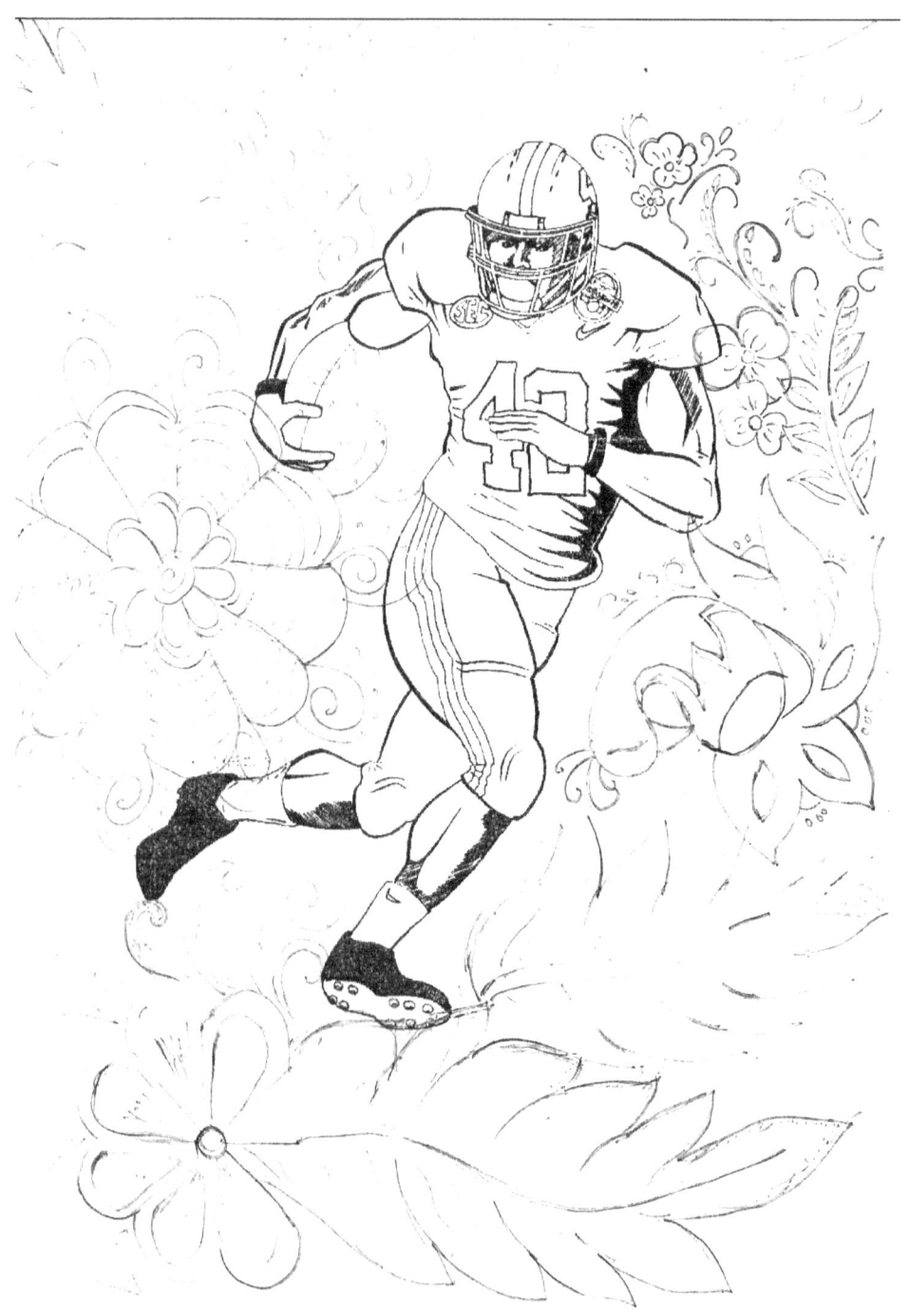

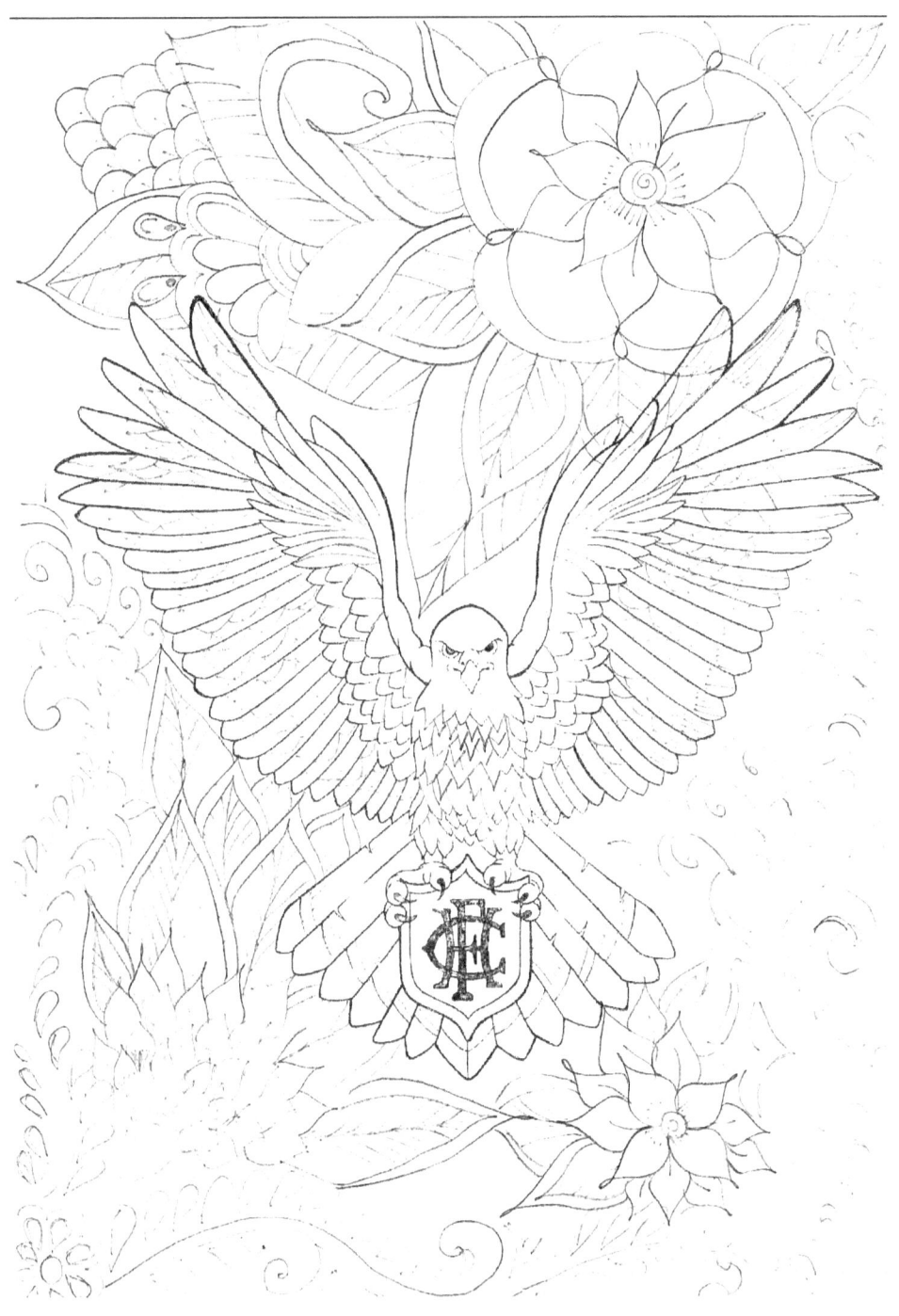

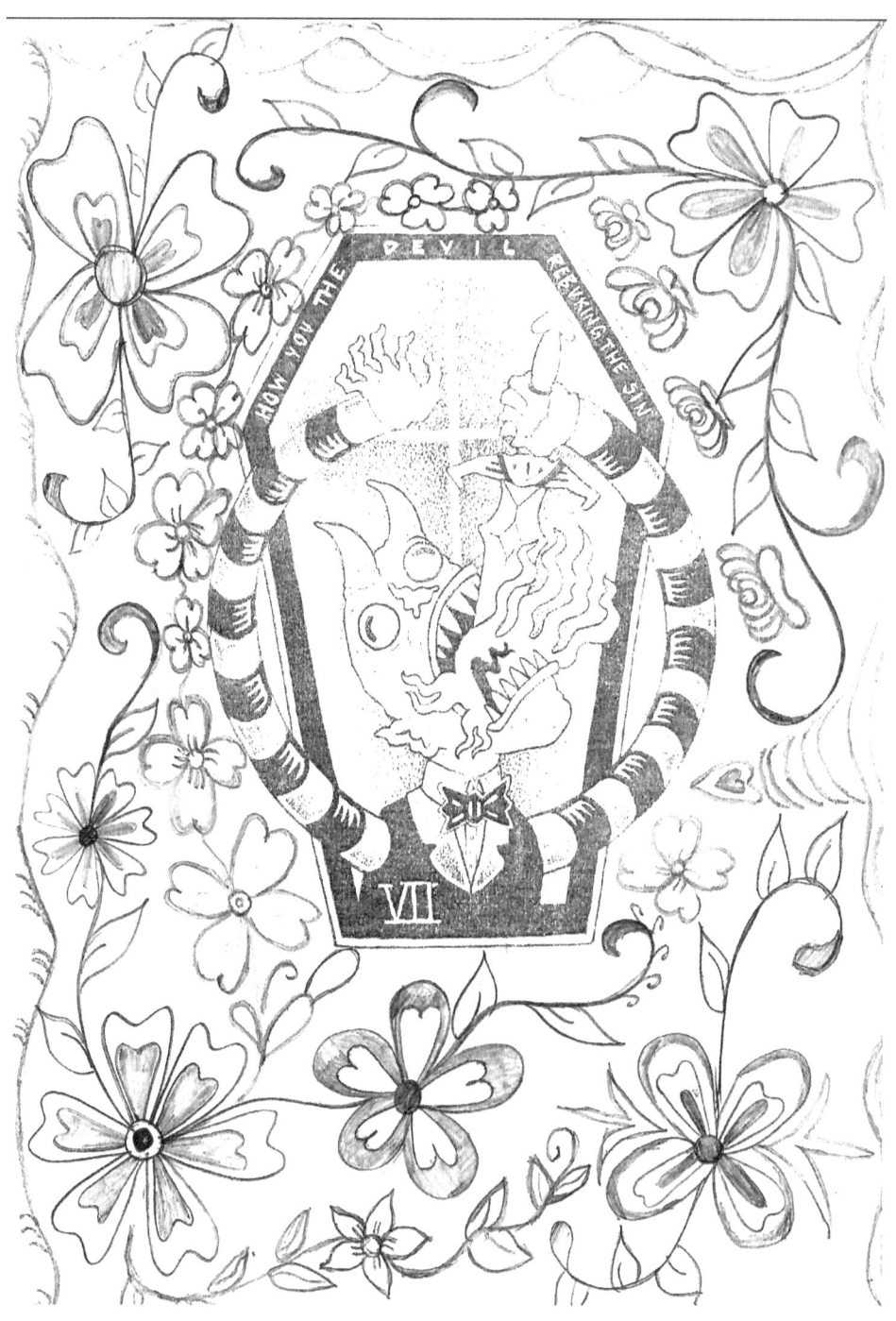

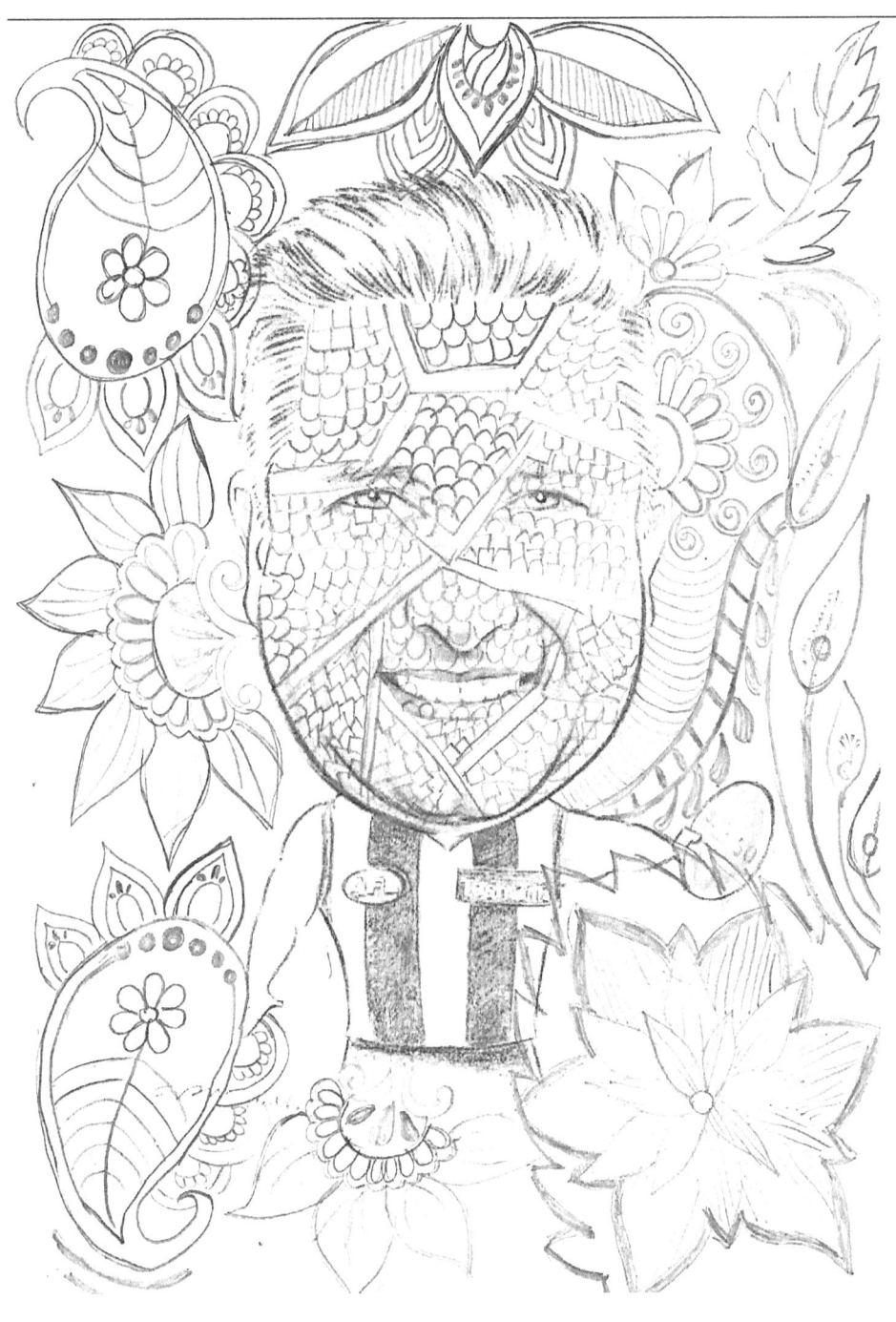

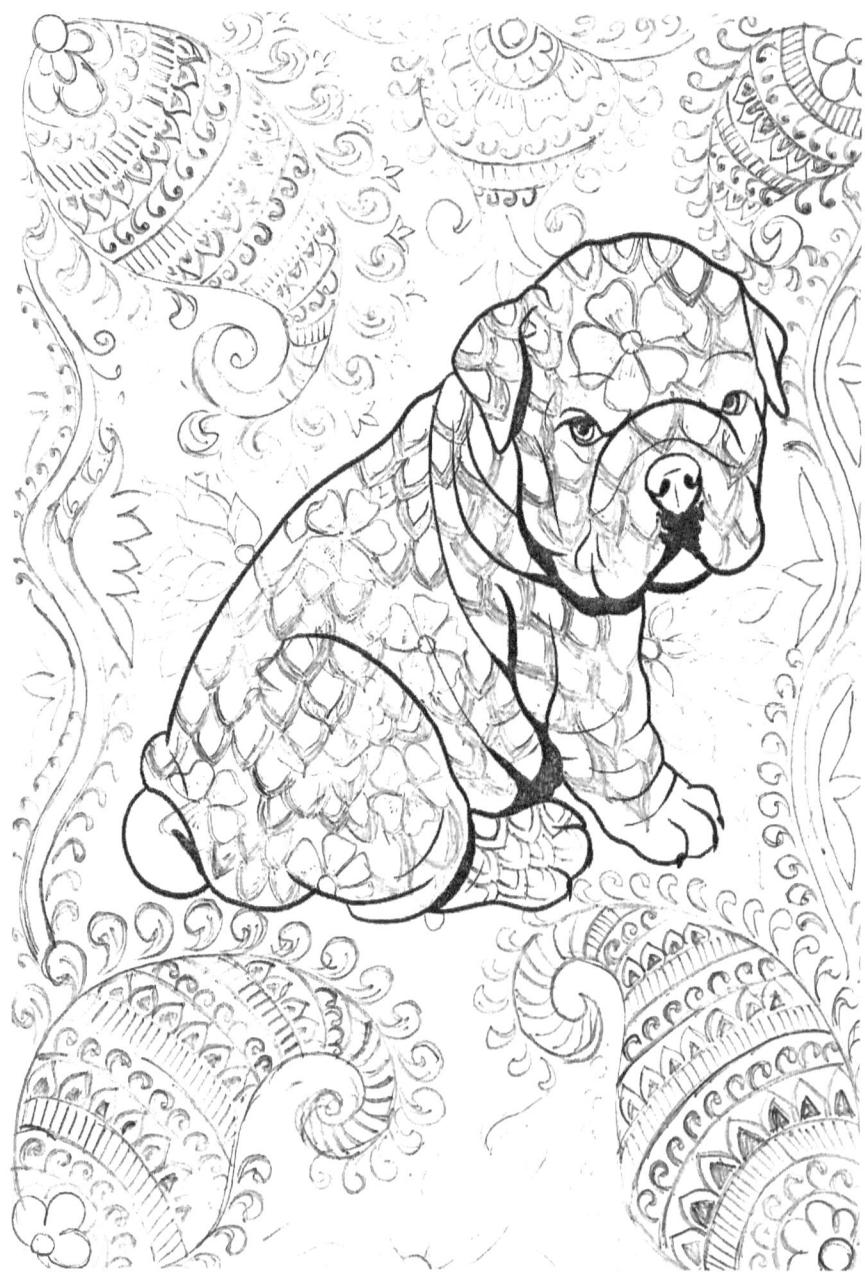

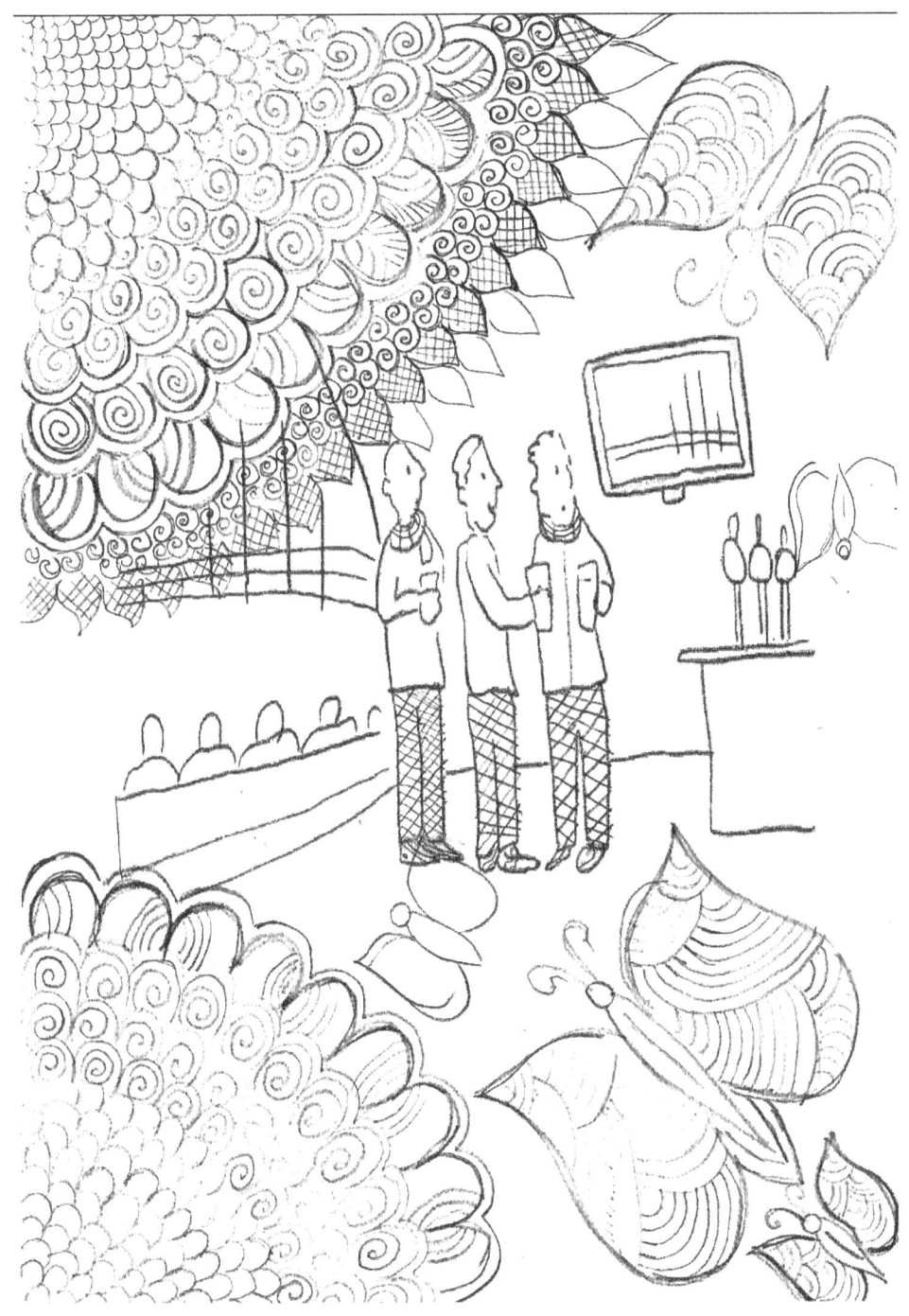

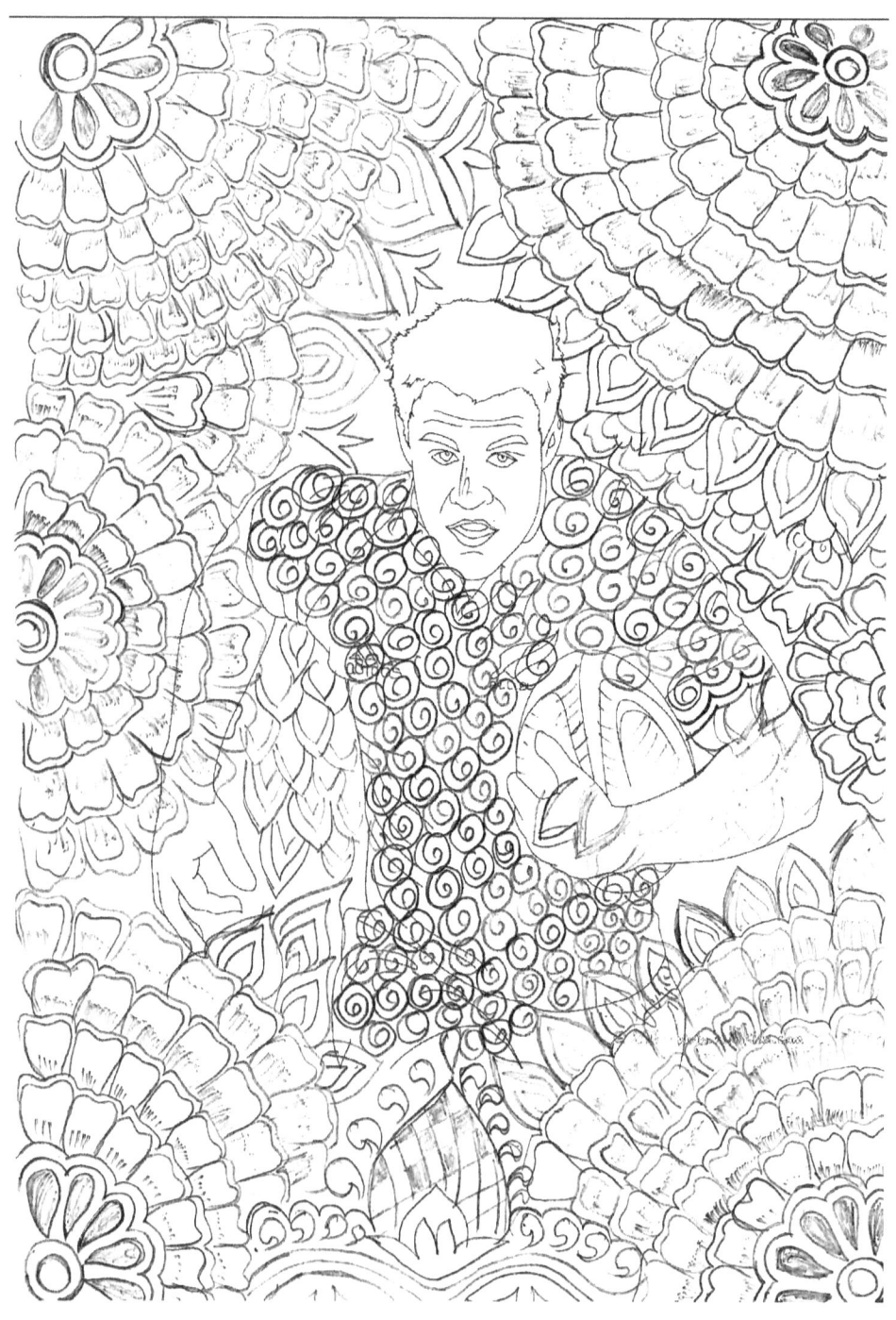

About Author

Emily Magic is author of bestselling The Footie Coloring Book. If you would like to publish this book in a different language, please feel free to contact author's secretary at

johntrumpet_@outlook.com